MW01234175

Cultivating Godliness

An Eight-Week Bible Study
In 1-2 Chronicles

Carol M. Kaminski

ISBN: 979-8-9867285-5-1

The artwork for the cover has been created by Amanda Mittelman. The floral and botanical design is intended to evoke Edenic imagery found in the Jerusalem Temple, recalling that the walls and doors of the temple were embellished with carvings of gourds, open flowers, palm trees, and ornamental pomegranates (1 Kgs. 6:1-38; 2 Chr. 3–4).

Contents

Introduction · 1

Week 1: Getting to Know Chronicles · · · · · · · · · · · · 9
Week 2: Praying to God · · · · · · · · · · · · · · · · · · · 21
Week 3: Seeking God · 33
Week 4: Humbling Oneself · · · · · · · · · · · · · · · · · 45
Week 5: Listening to Wise Counsel · · · · · · · · · · · · · 57
Week 6: Seeking God's Help · · · · · · · · · · · · · · · · 71
Week 7: Giving Generously · · · · · · · · · · · · · · · · · 85
Week 8: Singing Joyfully to God · · · · · · · · · · · · · · 99

Guidelines for Leaders · 113

Introduction

The title for this Bible study is *Cultivating Godliness*. The term *cultivate* has the sense of taking steps to grow or develop, suggesting that effort will be required on our part if we are to experience spiritual growth. The term *godliness* refers to every aspect of the Christian life. Since we are considering what godliness means *in Chronicles*, the goal of our study is to cultivate godly habits and virtues that align with God's kingdom, as reflected in the lives of Israel's kings and in the covenant community. God has set apart his people to be a worshiping and witnessing people among the nations. That a *holy* God dwells among his people means that their practices will look decidedly different than the surrounding nations. They belong to the kingdom of God, and as such, godly habits and virtues in Chronicles include prayer, seeking God's face, humbling oneself, listening to wise counsel, crying out to God for help, generosity, and singing to the Lord. These theologically rich topics are central to our walk with the Lord, and Chronicles will help us reflect on them.

As you begin this study, you may be tempted to think that Chronicles is simply a history book that "chronicles" Israel's kings, with minimal relevance for the topic of *godliness*. Given that Chronicles begins with nine chapters of genealogies (!), perhaps you have read 1-2 Kings as your Old Testament "history lesson." Sadly, Chronicles is one of the most neglected books in the Old Testament. I can still remember the time when someone asked me about my writing project while I was on sabbatical. I answered, "Chronicles," without giving it further thought. The person responded: "Do you mean the Chronicles *of Narnia*?" "No, I'm referring to Chronicles *in the Bible*."

Reflect for a moment with me. When was the last time you heard a preaching series or read a devotional on Chronicles? Regrettably, we skip over this portion of Scripture and look for something more interesting, and shall we say, more relevant. So, why study Chronicles? We could of course recall Paul's words to Timothy that all Scripture "is inspired by God and profitable for teaching, for reproof, for correction, for training in righteousness" (2 Tim. 3:16; cf. Rom. 15:4). Paul's reference to "all Scripture" surely includes Chronicles. It serves as a reminder that Chronicles *is* profitable for training in godliness.

Spiritual Lessons in Chronicles

In this study you will learn that Chronicles is a deeply spiritual book. You may be surprised to learn that Chronicles is all about prayer, trusting in God, worship, and especially, seeking God's face. Reading and applying the lessons taught in Chronicles will help you to cultivate godliness in your own life, and you will grow deeper in your relationship with the Lord. This is what happened in my own life after spending many years writing a commentary on 1-2 Chronicles. Be prepared for what God has in store for you—for he promises to be found by those who seek him!

Chronicles was written to call God's people back to the essentials of the faith. The author of Chronicles (more about him shortly) is retelling Israel's familiar stories of their kings. He is a gifted storyteller and preacher, writing during a difficult period in Israel's history. Under the sovereign hand of God, the Holy Spirit directs him to draw out spiritual lessons from the lives of Israel's kings that apply to God's people throughout the ages. The returnees living in Jerusalem were to lift their eyes beyond their immediate circumstances and gain a fresh vision of their sacred calling that hearkens back to God's original intention for creation. They were to understand that they were first and foremost citizens of God's kingdom (not the Persian Empire!) and that their lives were to be characterized by prayer and joyful worship. God's people were to cultivate godly practices that were central to their calling to be a worshiping and witnessing people among the nations. Life was not easy for those living in Jerusalem after the exile, but godliness is not simply to be cultivated when things are going well. As is often the case, adversity causes people to reflect on what is important. God uses these times to draw his people into a deeper relationship with him, and this is what he is doing with the returnees living in Jerusalem.

The Origin of Kingship in Genesis

As we begin learning about Israel's kings, it's important to remember that kingship is first found in the book of Genesis when God promised Abraham and Sarah that kings would come forth from their line (Gen. 17:6, 16). In accordance with God's promise, Sarah had miraculously given birth to a son named Isaac (Gen. 21), and the line had continued through Isaac's son Jacob, who fathered twelve sons (Gen. 35:22b-26). But the promised *royal* line would be taken up by Jacob's fourth-born son, Judah (Gen. 49:8-10). Hundreds of years later, kingship is on the horizon when the prophet Samuel anoints a shepherd boy in Bethlehem to be king over Israel. Even though he is the youngest in his family, David is anointed as God's chosen king from the royal line of Judah (1 Sam. 16). Chronicles tells the stories of Israel's kings from the line of Judah who rule on David's throne in Jerusalem. You are probably familiar with well-known kings like David and Solomon, but there are other important kings whose stories are less familiar to us. In this Bible study you will learn about godly kings, like Asa, Jehoshaphat, Hezekiah, and Josiah, but also about ungodly kings like Ahaz, Manasseh, and Zedekiah. Their stories, and many more, are told in 1-2 Chronicles over an extensive sixty-five chapters. Learning about godly kings and how God's people respond during difficult and challenging circumstances will help us cultivate godliness in our own lives and in our church communities. My prayer is that God will stir in you a love for these delightful stories of Israel's kings, and that through your study of the Scriptures, you will draw nearer to God and be more closely aligned with his heavenly kingdom.

Artwork on the Cover

The beautifully designed cover depicts flora and lush plant life native to the land of Israel. The botanical imagery is intended to evoke the temple in Jerusalem, recalling that the walls and doors of the temple were embellished with carvings of gourds, open flowers, palm trees, and ornamental pomegranates (1 Kgs. 6:1-38; 2 Chr. 3–4). These beautiful carvings, along with luminous gold and precious stones, signal to the imagination that the temple is sacred space, reminiscent of the Garden of Eden. The glorious temple in Jerusalem is central to the book of Chronicles, and throughout our study we will be drawn to it in prayer and worship. The cover is intended to evoke the beauty of the temple, and it invites us to draw near to God.

Cultivating Godliness in Community

As we begin our study, it is important to recognize that we live in a highly individualized society. When reading the title, *Cultivating Godliness,* your first instinct may have been to think of your personal relationship with God. While there is clearly a personal dimension to godliness in Chronicles, especially as we look at the lives of individual kings, we need to keep in mind that Israel's kings were not solo leaders. The king's character was shaped *by others*—God intends it this way. Spiritual counselors, bold prophets, and wise teachers are given to the king to keep him on a godly path. This reminds us that *our* character is shaped by those around us, and that we, too, can be a godly influence on the lives of others. God has put his Spirit in each one of us, and he uses others in our church community to keep us on a godly path—we need each other!

As we dig deeper into the Scriptures, our rugged individualism and self-reliance will be exposed so that we might learn to rely on God. We too easily take pride in our ability to multi-task and get a job done. The inherent danger of this "can do" attitude is that we become self-reliant, and even prideful in what *we* can accomplish. Yet this adversely affects our relationship with fellow believers since our self-reliance isolates us from each other. The stories of Israel's kings demonstrate that strength, success, and wealth can lead to pride, self-reliance, and a failure to seek God. In Chronicles we watch the tragic demise of kings who begin with all the hallmarks of godliness but finish poorly as they rely on their own strength and accomplishments instead of trusting in God. Their lives serve as a reminder that godliness needs to be cultivated daily and throughout the entirety of our lives. But there's even more to these stories, as they teach us that godliness is nurtured and expressed in the covenant community. In this study we will learn about kings like Jehoshaphat and Josiah, who seek the face of God, but there are times when the entire community seeks God *together*. Similarly, individual kings, such as David and Hezekiah, demonstrate generosity, but there is great joy when generosity is shown by the entire community. The king's generosity stirs others to be generous. This means that *together* we are called to cultivate godly habits in our lives, and that our presence can nurture spiritual growth in others. Self-reliant individuals do not finish well on this path of godliness, but God has given us brothers and sisters on the journey so that we can encourage each other in our walk with the Lord.

Keeping this communal aspect of godliness in mind, weekly Bible readings and questions are designed to be done individually at home, yet they are intended to be shared in a weekly small group. We belong to one body, the church, and we need each other to grow in our relationship with God so that we might walk faithfully with him. God is glorified in our individual lives, to be sure, but we are called to be a worshiping and witnessing community, reflecting God's character to the world. This is something we do *together*. My presence matters because I belong to one body under the Lordship of Jesus.

Weekly Bible Readings and Questions

Four to five chapters from Chronicles have been assigned each week for the Bible readings. I would recommend that you set aside thirty minutes each day reading one biblical passage and answering the corresponding questions. When verses are quoted in this Bible study, they may be slightly different than the version you are using. Don't be put off by this. The New American Standard Bible (NASB) has been cited in this study, but there are other trustworthy English translations, such as the New International Version (NIV) or the English Standard Version (ESV). Use a Bible that you are familiar with, and you may even want to underline key verses that stand out to you. Sometimes you will be reading biblical passages that you have studied a few weeks earlier, but different questions will be asked. Reading the same chapter will enable you to dig deeper and notice new things that you may not have seen earlier, and it will reinforce important lessons from previous weeks. If you have extra time, it is always beneficial to read the chapter that comes before the assigned biblical passage so that you have a sense of where you are in the story. In this study you will be asked several questions on each chapter that relate to content and application. Ask the Holy Spirit to guide you in your Bible readings and be open to hear what God might be saying to you through the Scriptures. The goal of the weekly readings is not simply information but transformation. This happens as we encounter the Lord in the Scriptures and respond in obedience to his word, as his Spirit stirs our heart and opens our mind.

Bible Study for Women

It is my hope that this Bible study will be used by women in the church. Too often women's Bible studies are not theologically rigorous, but there are many women who take the Bible seriously and who want in-depth Bible studies. I hope this study provides a theologically rich Bible study for these women, though it has not been written exclusively for women. We all need to learn from this theologically rich book, and we all need to cultivate godliness. Ideally, a preaching series could accompany this Bible study, following the eight-week outline. This would reinforce key topics presented in the weekly studies, and it would ensure that this important yet neglected book is taught from the pulpit. This is my prayer as I write this Bible study.

Commentary on 1-2 Chronicles

As you embark on this study, I hope that your interest in Chronicles will be piqued and that you take the step to study it in more depth. I would recommend my commentary on 1-2 Chronicles entitled: *1-2 Chronicles. Story of God Bible Commentary* (eds. Tremper Longman III and Scot McKnight; Grand Rapids: Zondervan, 2023). The commentary includes sections on authorship, historical context, literary structure, and theological themes. An in-depth analysis is given for each chapter of 1-2 Chronicles, which will complement the Bible readings assigned for this study. The best way to use this resource is to read the commentary sections on the chapters assigned for the weekly Bible readings. At the end of each chapter in the commentary, areas for application are highlighted in the section entitled, "Live the Story." Since the commentary's focus is on the story of God, it will not only enrich your weekly Bible readings but help you keep the storyline in focus. You may even decide to read the commentary from cover to cover, which will only enhance your study of Chronicles. Important theological themes found in Chronicles are highlighted throughout the commentary, which include many of the topics we will be exploring in this Bible study. If you are leading this Bible study, you'll want to read the Leader's Guide at the end of this volume, but I would also encourage you to read the relevant sections in my commentary.

My prayer is that as you study Chronicles, you will discover the richness of God's word and the treasures to be found in these beloved stories. In our age of restlessness and transience, we can easily move from one pursuit to the next, always pursuing but never fully finding. But God is inviting us through Chronicles to seek his face, and he promises to be found by those who seek him. Take time to reflect on God's word. Take time to pray and seek his face. Set your eyes on *him*. This is the journey God has set before us—a journey we take *together*.

WEEK 1

Getting to Know Chronicles

Location of 1-2 Chronicles in the Bible

Let's get started with locating 1-2 Chronicles in the list of Old Testament books. It would be helpful for you to open your Bible to the Table of Contents. You will notice that Chronicles is listed as two separate books, known as 1 and 2 Chronicles or first and second Chronicles. 1-2 Chronicles has been placed immediately after 1-2 Kings. The first five books of the Old Testament (Genesis-Deuteronomy) are known as the Torah ("law, instruction") or the Pentateuch ("five-fold volume"). The next group is known as the Historical Books (Joshua-Esther), and 1-2 Chronicles is included among them. It is important to keep in mind that the order of Old Testament books is not according to chronology but genre (type of literature). 1-2 Chronicles has been placed with 1-2 Samuel and 1-2 Kings because they are all books about Israel's history, even though 1-2 Chronicles was written in the final period of the Old Testament, closer to the time of Ezra, Nehemiah, Esther, and Malachi. In the Hebrew Bible, 1-2 Chronicles occurs at the end of the third division of books, known as the Writings ("Ketuvim").

Literary Structure of the Book

It is important to gain a sense of the literary structure of 1-2 Chronicles, as it will help you navigate your way through the stories of Israel's kings. First Chronicles opens with nine chapters of genealogies (most of the tribes of Israel are represented), which emphasize the unity of the tribes. By beginning with Adam, the genealogies communicate that God's plan for his creation is being fulfilled through all Israel (1 Chr. 1–9). The genealogies are followed by one chapter on King Saul (1 Chr. 10), along with nineteen chapters on King David (1 Chr. 11–29). The length of material devoted to David underscores that he is the most important king in 1 Chronicles. This beloved king holds a special place in Israel's traditions. Second Chronicles begins with the reign of David's son Solomon, another important king who is especially known for his construction of the temple in Jerusalem (2 Chr. 1–9). The kingdom divides into two in 930 BC when Solomon's son Rehoboam becomes king. The remaining chapters in 2 Chronicles cover the divided kingdom, with focus on Davidic kings who rule in Jerusalem (2 Chr. 10–36).

Kingship in the Old Testament

Chronicles recalls the stories of Israel's kings from Saul to Zedekiah, covering almost five hundred years of history (1050-586 BC). It is important to bear in mind that about one thousand years before King David, God had promised Abraham and Sarah that kings would come from them (Gen. 17:6, 15-16). This promise will be realized through their great-grandson, Judah. At the end of the book of Genesis, a prophetic word spoken by Jacob pronounces that Judah's brothers will "praise" him (a play on Judah's name, "he will be praised," Gen. 49:8; cf. 29:35) and that the "scepter will not depart from Judah" (Gen. 49:10). This identifies kingship with Jacob's fourth born son, Judah. Since Jacob's sons become tribal leaders, the prophetic word locates the promised royal line with the tribe of Judah. It is not surprising to find, therefore, that the genealogy of the tribe of Judah is one of the longest genealogies in Chronicles—it is because God's chosen king (and the coming Messiah) will come from this tribe (1 Chr. 2:3–3:24). You may want to take a few moments to read the passages from Genesis noted above and underline them in your Bible, as they form the background for the story of kingship in the Old Testament.

With this prophetic blessing on Judah in view, a young shepherd boy named David from the tribe of Judah is anointed king by the prophet Samuel (1 Sam. 16). This takes place in David's hometown of Bethlehem, a city located within the tribal allotment of Judah. Yet David will not become king until after the death of Saul, at which time God turns the kingdom over to him (1 Chr. 10). The importance of David's reign is underscored by the fact that nineteen chapters are devoted to him (1 Chr. 11–29). Every king ruling in Jerusalem after David is from his lineage, and his line will finally lead to the Messiah (Matt. 1:1-17). Given the importance of David, it is not surprising that "Bethlehem" is mentioned in the genealogies (1 Chr. 2:51, 54; 4:4) and that messianic expectations will be centered on this town (Mic. 5:2; cf. Matt. 2:4-6; Luke 2:4). God promises David that he will raise up his son after him and establish his everlasting throne and kingdom (2 Sam. 7:8-17; 1 Chr. 17:1-15). I would encourage you to read the passages noted in this section and underline key Davidic promises found in 2 Samuel 7 and 1 Chronicles 17.

The next important person in the story of kingship is David's son, Solomon, who is chosen by God to build the temple in Jerusalem. The Chronicler gives considerable attention to the temple, along with Solomon's prayer of dedication (2 Chr. 2–7). In this portion of Scripture, we find the well-known verse from Chronicles: "If my people who are called by My name humble themselves and pray and seek My face and turn from their wicked ways, I will hear from heaven, will forgive their sin and will heal their land" (2 Chr. 7:14). This is the theme verse for our Bible study since it encapsulates many of the important topics found in Chronicles, such as humbling oneself, prayer, seeking God, repentance, and forgiveness. You may even want to commit this verse to memory. Solomon's reign is recorded in 2 Chr. 1–9, but after he dies, the kingdom divides into two because of God's judgment against him for his idolatry (2 Chr. 10:1-19). As a result, ten tribes move to the north under the leadership of a military leader named Jeroboam, but the tribes of Judah, Benjamin, and Levi remain in the south under the leadership of Solomon's son, Rehoboam.

The Chronicler tells the stories of the southern kings ruling in Jerusalem after the division, with special attention given to kings like Asa, Jehoshaphat, Hezekiah, and Josiah. Every king in the south is from the tribe of Judah, and the kingdom is marked by dynastic succession. But kingship comes to a tragic end in 586 BC when God's people are taken into exile to Babylon for their repeated failure to obey God's laws (2 Chr. 36). Although the story of kingship comes to an end, God's promises still stand. The prophets announce that God will raise up a righteous king in fulfillment of his promises to David (e.g., Jer. 23:5-6; 33:15-17). Even though there is no king on the throne during the final period of the Old Testament, the Davidic line continues beyond the exile (1 Chr. 3:17-24), and it will ultimately lead to the birth of the Messiah (Matt. 1:12-17). As you study Chronicles, you will discover that the book reverberates with messianic hope, and even the final verses end with the call to return to Jerusalem (2 Chr. 36:22-23). This hopeful message is because of God's enduring promises that await their certain fulfilment—God is faithful!

The Old Testament CASKET EMPTY Timeline

Learning about Israel's kings can be confusing, especially during the period of the divided kingdom. But it is important to be able to identify the historical context for the king you are studying. The best way to do this is to have a visual timeline in front of you. The *CASKET EMPTY Old Testament Timeline* that I have created traces the storyline of the Old Testament through six key periods, using the acronym CASKET. The period of Kings on the timeline (represented by the letter K in the CASKET acronym) will be invaluable as you read about Israel's kings in Chronicles. Concise summaries are given for each king on the timeline, which will help you identify the character of the king and important events in his reign. You'll also be able to see whether a king is northern or southern since the two kingdoms are represented visually on the timeline. If you are unfamiliar with CASKET EMPTY, the word CASKET is an acronym for the Old Testament (Creation, Abraham, Sinai, Kings, Exile, and Temple) and the word EMPTY is an acronym for the New Testament (Expectations, Messiah, Pentecost, Teachings, and Yet-to-come). The title CASKET EMPTY® serves as a reminder that the death and resurrection of Jesus are at the center of God's plan of redemption in the Bible. The timeline is available through the Casket Empty website (www.casketempty.com).

Hebrew Words

In this study you'll notice that Hebrew words are mentioned from time to time. The Old Testament was originally written in Hebrew (with a few chapters in Aramaic), and the New Testament was written in Greek. You are not expected to know these original languages, but sometimes it is helpful to refer to specific Hebrew words, as they provide a more in-depth understanding of a particular passage. Hebrew words have been given in *transliteration*, which simply means that words are written with English letters that sound like the original Hebrew word. Although some of the letters are slightly different (such as the letter š, which in Hebrew sounds more like *sh*), the benefit of transliteration is that you'll be able to refer to a Hebrew word by reading the English.

Who Wrote Chronicles?

The author of Chronicles is unknown to us because his name is not mentioned anywhere in the book. One view is that Ezra wrote Chronicles. You'll notice that the final verses of 2 Chronicles are almost identical to the opening verses of Ezra (2 Chr. 36:22-23; Ezra 1:1-3). This could indicate that the same person wrote both books. Furthermore, since Chronicles and Ezra were both written in the final period of the Old Testament, and since Ezra was a Levite skilled in the law of Moses (Ezra 7:6), he is certainly a good candidate for authorship. However, more recent scholarship has demonstrated that Ezra and Chronicles have too many differences in language, literary style, and theology to be written by the same person. It is more likely that the person who wrote Chronicles did not write Ezra, although he was probably a Levite, like Ezra, who devoted himself to the study of the Scriptures. Since we do not know the author's name, we must be content to call him "the Chronicler."

When Was Chronicles Written?

Chronicles was written during the final period of the Old Testament, known, as the Persian Period, when God's people were ruled by foreign Persian kings. You may recall that they had gone into exile in 586 BC because of their failure to uphold God's laws, but God had promised to restore his people. In 539 BC, the Persian king Cyrus defeats Babylon, and in accordance with the prior prophecy of Isaiah (Isa. 44–45), he issues a decree, allowing God's people to return to Jerusalem and rebuild the temple. The first group of exiles returns to Jerusalem in 538 BC under the leadership of Sheshbazzar, governor of Judah, and rebuilding of the temple begins. After some initial setbacks, the temple is rebuilt in 516 BC under the leadership of Zerubbabel (grandson of Jehoiachin) and Joshua (the high priest), with the encouragement of Haggai and Zechariah. If you would like to learn more about the first return from exile, you could read Ezra 1–6, along with the prophets Haggai and Zechariah. A second group of exiles returns to Jerusalem in 458 BC under the leadership of Ezra the priest. Covenant renewal takes place, and the walls of Jerusalem are rebuilt under the leadership of Nehemiah, governor of Judah. If you would like to learn more about the second return from exile and the events that follow, you could read Ezra 7–10, Nehemiah, and Malachi. The Chronicler is writing in this final period of the Old Testament, which is dated to the fifth century BC.

Life in the Province of Judah

God's people return to Jerusalem and rebuild the temple, but during this period they are living within the small province of Judah (known as *Yehud*) amid a vast Persian Empire ruled by foreign kings. God had promised David that his descendant would rule over God's everlasting kingdom, yet at this time, God's people are waiting for God to fulfill what he has promised. This means that there is no king from the tribe of Judah on the throne, but instead, Persian kings rule vast regions of the ancient Near East. Their realm is divided into provinces under the jurisdiction of local governors (Ezra 5:6, 14; Neh. 5:14-15; cf. Esth. 1:1). The province of *Yehud* was much smaller than the flourishing kingdom under David and Solomon. The returnees who live in Jerusalem and in the surrounding towns face opposition from foreign nations, which include Samaritans to the north, Edomites to the south, Ammonites to the east, and Phoenicians to the west. Some among the returnees had faced dire poverty, requiring them to mortgage their property. They were paying heavy taxes to the Persian government and prices of basic commodities were highly inflated. God's people were in danger of compromising with the surrounding nations (and potentially even adopting their religious beliefs; cf. Ezra 9–10). This is a far cry from the glory days of the kingdom under David and Solomon, yet this is precisely why these stories written by the Chronicler are so important.

God is teaching his people what it means to live as citizens of *his kingdom*, even though their own lives were filled with struggles and uncertainties. God had set apart his people to be a worshiping and witnessing people among the nations—and this vision still stands. Amid a time of uncertainty and transition, God's people were to cultivate godly habits and to keep their eyes fixed on the kingdom. It is not surprising to find that topics like prayer, seeking God's face, reliance upon God, and even generosity reverberate throughout Chronicles. The message of this book is relevant for our lives today. Like God's people of old, we, too, need to cultivate godliness and keep our eyes fixed on God's kingdom. When we face struggles, challenges, and uncertainties, what do we do? Do we "toughen up" and simply "pull up our bootstraps," or do we turn to God in prayer and put our trust in him? When we face insurmountable obstacles, we are exhorted in Chronicles to set our face to seek the Lord. We are to lift our eyes beyond our immediate circumstances and gain a fresh vision of God's heavenly kingdom. Like a delightful recurring melody, the Levites will draw us into worship, stirring our hearts to sing praises to our God. My prayer is that as you study Chronicles, songs of praise might arise in your heart and that you might gain a fresh vision of God's everlasting kingdom.

Conversation Starters

1. In this study we will learn about Israel's kings in the Old Testament, but since this portion of Scripture may be unfamiliar to you, this can feel rather intimidating. What areas might intimidate you or excite you about this study in Chronicles? Check as many as you like!

   ☐ I haven't read the Old Testament, so I really don't know even the basics—I'll need some help!

   ☐ I'm embarrassed that others will know more about the Bible than I do.

   ☐ I'm a new Christian, so *everything* is new to me.

   ☐ I'm struggling in my personal life, so I'm nervous about being vulnerable with others.

   ☐ I love the Old Testament, so I'm excited about studying Chronicles!

   ☐ Other _____

2. Spend time perusing 1-2 Chronicles, noting some of the headings in your Bible. What is your first impression of Chronicles? Is there anything that stands out to you?

3. When you think of the word "godliness," what qualities come to mind?

4. Identify a godly person who has had a positive influence in your own life. What stood out to you in this person's life? How did this person influence you?

5. Chronicles was written to people who were facing difficulties and uncertainties. Identify a time in your life when your struggles or difficulties caused you to turn to God in prayer and rely upon him. What did God teach you during this time?

6. What is your greatest strength and how might this cause you to rely on yourself instead of God?

7. What do you hope to learn in this study? Are there any specific "godly habits" you would like to cultivate? Ask God to help you and give him any concerns that you have.

Praying to God

We begin our study by reflecting on the important topic of prayer, seen especially in the extended prayer of Solomon when the temple is dedicated. Prayer is, in fact, one of the main themes in Chronicles. This should not surprise us since difficult circumstances often cause people to turn to God for help. The theme of prayer reverberates throughout Chronicles as a testimony that God hears and answers prayers, and it will be instructive for our prayer lives. During Old Testament times, God's people could offer prayers to him at any time and at any place (as Manasseh does, for example, when he prays in Babylon), but the temple had a central role in the corporate prayer life of ancient Israel. About four hundred years before Solomon builds the temple in Jerusalem, God had instructed Moses to build a tabernacle so that he might dwell with his people and meet with them there (Exod. 25:8, 22; 29:43, 46). The book of Exodus describes the construction of the tabernacle with its elaborate and costly furnishings, and it concludes with God's glory filling it (Exod. 25–40). When the Israelites leave Sinai and journey toward the promised land, the Levites are assigned the sacred task of moving the tabernacle, as the glory-cloud leads them (Num. 9:15-23). When David becomes king over all Israel, he plans to build a glorious temple for God in Jerusalem (the place chosen by God as the sacred site), but it is made known to him through the prophet Nathan that his son Solomon will build it (1 Chr. 17:11-12; 22:6-11; 28:2-7). In preparation for this task, David generously gives his gold, silver, and precious resources to be used in its construction (1 Chr. 22, 28–29). When Solomon becomes king, he spends seven years building a magnificent and glorious temple that is beautifully decorated and lavishly adorned with gold and precious stones reminiscent of the Garden of Eden (2 Chr. 2–5; cf. Gen. 2–3). Artisans are employed from the coastal region of Phoenicia to ensure that the temple is worthy of Israel's God. Botanical and arboreal imagery signal to the imagination that the temple is a microcosm of creation itself, an earthly replica of God's heavenly abode. As noted earlier, the cover design for this Bible study is intended to evoke the Jerusalem Temple, which was embellished with carvings of gourds, open lily flowers, palm trees and pomegranates, signifying an Edenic garden (see 2 Chr. 3–5). The temple is the life-giving center of the entire community. It is the place where worship is offered daily to the LORD who dwells among his people. Priests and Levites officiate at the temple and represent Israel before a holy God.

Yet the temple is not simply an ornate building, but it is the place of God's presence. God's glory dwells above the Edenic cherubim that flank the ark of the covenant located in the Holy of Holies (2 Chr. 5:7-14; 7:1-3). Construction of the temple under Solomon marks a climactic moment in the story of redemption in the Old Testament because a holy God dwells among his people. This is why it is so important. It is God's *presence* that distinguishes Israel from the surrounding nations. The Chronicler has taken considerable time to describe the construction of the temple (2 Chr. 2–5), yet the narrative does not conclude with the completed building. It concludes with *prayer*—the temple is the place where the LORD, who is gloriously enthroned in heaven, descends to meet with his people. This week we are invited to meditate on Solomon's extended prayer of dedication (2 Chr. 6). The temple narrative resounds with the profound reality that God desires to have fellowship with his people.

In the Bible readings this week, you will encounter King Solomon at the dedication of the temple, kneeling on a large bronze platform with uplifted hands toward heaven. This is a sacred moment as the king communes with his God. This is the place where heaven and earth meet. Solomon prays to the *living* God, and in this story, we learn the remarkable truth that God hears and answers prayer. He further instructs his people about prayer, teaching them to humble themselves, pray and seek his face, and he promises to hear from heaven, forgive, and heal (2 Chr. 7:14). Throughout Solomon's prayer, God's people are exhorted to pray and to make supplication before God in the temple (2 Chr. 6:24). Given the chapter's emphasis on prayer, it is not surprising to find that prayers are rehearsed elsewhere in Chronicles (2 Chr. 30:18; 32:20, 24; 33:13). The vital role of prayer is exemplified in the lives of kings such as Hezekiah, when he prays to God amid a national crisis (2 Chr. 32:20-22), and Manasseh, when he prays to God while in distress in Babylon (2 Chr. 33:12-13, 19). These are just two of the stories the Chronicler highlights, but many others could be mentioned during this final period of the Old Testament (see Ezra 8:21-23; 9:5-15; 10:1; Neh. 1:4-11; 2:4; 4:9; 6:9; 9:1-37). Although we no longer pray in the temple (Jesus has established a new and living way into God's presence; see Heb. 10:19-25), these prayers are instructive for us so that we might learn *how* to pray and be encouraged that God hears and answers prayer. As you read the biblical passages this week, take time to pray and enjoy fellowship with the Lord, who is present in our lives through the indwelling of his Spirit.

ℬ𝒾𝒷𝓁𝑒 𝑅𝑒𝒶𝒹𝒾𝓃𝑔𝓈

1 Chronicles 17:1-27; 29:1-22; 2 Chronicles 6:1-42; 7:1-14; 20:1-13

𝒬𝓊𝑒𝓈𝓉𝒾𝑜𝓃𝓈 𝒻𝑜𝓇 𝑅𝑒𝒻𝓁𝑒𝒸𝓉𝒾𝑜𝓃

1. Read 1 Chronicles 17. We begin our study of prayer with King David. God makes promises to him that are central to the storyline of the entire Bible (you should have underlined them in your Bible by now, 1 Chr. 17:1-15). We pick up the story with David's response, when he sits before his God in prayer (vv. 16-27). This is not a public event but an intimate moment of fellowship. As you read David's prayer, what stands out to you?

2. How does David begin his prayer and what is his posture before God (vv. 16-19)? What is unique about the LORD and what past actions of God does David recall (vv. 20-22)?

3. As you reflect on your own life, what things has God done that cause you to praise him? How might God's past actions encourage you in your faith today and how might you encourage others in your group who may be struggling?

4. David petitions the LORD in his prayer (vv. 23-27). Summarize what David asks God to do. What is the focus of his prayer and what might you learn from it?

5. Read 1 Chronicles 29:1-22. David has walked with God from his youth, but his life on earth will shortly come to an end. How does his prayer at the end of his life compare with his earlier prayer (1 Chr. 17:16-27)? How would you describe David's relationship with God, even as he faces his own imminent death?

6. David's view of the transitory nature of life has impacted his use of his time, energy, and resources. How do you plan to use the remaining years God has given you? Are there any of your priorities that need to change so that they might be more closely aligned with God's kingdom? We read in the book of Acts that David died "after he had served the purpose of God in his own generation" (Acts 13:36). What is God's purpose for *your* life?

7. Read 2 Chronicles 6. This chapter is one of the jewels of Chronicles. Solomon's prayer of dedication is rich in theology. It serves as a "timeless prayer" for God's people throughout the ages. I would encourage you to read the chapter out loud in one sitting. What is your initial impression of Solomon's prayer? What stands out to you?

8. Notice Solomon's posture when he prays (v. 13). Kneeling before God in prayer reflects a posture of humility. In the Old Testament people often bow down before God in worship (2 Chr. 7:3; 20:18; 29:30), with uplifted hands (Neh. 8:6; cf. Pss. 28:2; 141:2). Sometimes people stand when praying (2 Chr. 20:5, 9, 13), which can include spreading out their hands before God (2 Chr. 6:13, 29). What gestures do you use in prayer or in worship? How might using a particular posture impact how you think of yourself and your relationship with God?

9. What aspect of God's character does Solomon highlight in his prayer? Why do you think he emphasizes what he does?

10. The verb "to pray" (*pālal*) occurs eight times in this chapter (vv. 19, 20, 21, 24, 26, 32, 34, 38). What is Solomon asking God to do in response to prayer? Make a list of the actions Solomon mentions (e.g., "listen," "forgive").

11. God's glory fills the newly constructed temple (2 Chr. 5:11-14; 7:1-3), but when Solomon prays, where does he locate God's dwelling place (6:18, 21, 23, 25, 27, etc.)? As Christians, we can pray to God at any time and at any place, whether in our home, on a walk, while driving, or anywhere else. What has happened in the redemptive story of the Bible so that we no longer need to pray *in the temple* (see John 4:21-24; 1 Cor. 3:16; Heb. 10:19-22)? How might this impact your own prayer life?

12. Read 2 Chronicles 7:1-14. God appears to Solomon at night and answers his prayer. In the first section (vv. 12-14), God reveals to Solomon the posture his people are to have before him, and he exhorts his people to pray and seek his face. God promises to hear from heaven, forgive, and heal the land. Taking this word to heart, the Chronicler highlights times when people humble themselves (2 Chr. 12:6-7; 30:11; 32:26; 33:12, 19; 34:27), pray (2 Chr. 30:18; 32:20, 24), and seek God (2 Chr. 11:16; 15:4, 15; 20:4). We will be studying these passages in the coming weeks, but for now, reflect on what God says in response to Solomon (vv. 12-14). In what way might God's word to Solomon be instructive for your own walk with the Lord?

13. 2 Chronicles 7:12-14 reminds us that God hears and answers prayer. In what way have you experienced answered prayer in your own life? How might this encourage you to have faith in God for your *current* circumstances?

14. One of the best ways to grow in your prayer life is to use a prayer journal (I've done this for the past thirty years). If you've never used a prayer journal, this would be a great time to begin! Perhaps those in your group who have used a prayer journal could share what they have found helpful. Using a prayer journal regularly provides an opportunity for you to write down your prayers and reflect on how God has worked in your life. Share in your group this week one habit or practice you have found helpful in your prayer life that might encourage others.

15. Read 2 Chronicles 20:1-13. We will be returning to this story in another lesson, but our focus this week is on prayer. How much of Jehoshaphat's prayer recalls God's character, attributes, past actions, and promises, and how much focuses on petition (asking God to do something)? In your own prayer life, how much of your prayers focus on God's character, attributes, past actions, and promises? How might Jehoshaphat's prayer encourage you to be more "God-focused" in your prayers?

16. Notice the role of the Spirit in response to Jehoshaphat's prayer. How would you describe the role of the Holy Spirit in your own life? How do we as Christians discern the activity of God's Spirit in our (individual) lives and in the church?

17. How do Jehoshaphat and the people demonstrate their faith in God? As Christians, we are called to walk by faith. Although the outcome might be uncertain, we are to put our trust in God. How does worship in this story *demonstrate* Israel's faith in God and how does it also *build* their faith?

18. Now that you have read through several prayers in Chronicles, list some of the common elements or themes you have noticed. What is one thing you could incorporate into your prayer life this week?

WEEK 3

Seeking God

Last week we studied the prayers of David (1 Chr. 17, 29), Solomon (2 Chr. 6), and Jehoshaphat (2 Chr. 20). You may recall from the story of Jehoshaphat that even before the king prayed, he "turned his attention to seek the Lord" (20:3). This week we will be exploring what it means to seek the Lord, which is central to the book of Chronicles. In fact, the Hebrew verb "to seek, inquire" (*dāraš,* sounds like *darash*) occurs more often in Chronicles than in any other Old Testament book. To illustrate this point, the verb occurs three times in 1-2 Samuel, thirteen times in 1-2 Kings, but over *forty* times in Chronicles. I mentioned in the Introduction that Chronicles is a spiritual book, and now you're beginning to see why. The stories of Israel's kings are not simply being told as a history lesson (even though they are historical accounts), but they provide examples of what it means to seek God, especially during difficult circumstances. Throughout these stories, God is exhorting his people to *seek him,* but what does this mean practically? Is seeking God the same as prayer or is it something else?

It is important to keep in mind that two different Hebrew verbs are used in Chronicles to describe seeking God. We've seen that the verb "to seek, inquire" (*dāraš*) appears frequently in Chronicles, but another verb translated as "seek" (*bāqaš,* sounds like *baqash*) is also used; this verb occurs thirteen times. In our study this week we will be reading about people who seek the LORD or inquire "of him." I will highlight which verb is used in each passage so that you can gain a deeper understanding of what it means to seek God. You will notice that sometimes both verbs appear together in the same passage.

We begin with the verb *dāraš*, which occurs outside of Chronicles. For example, it is used of Rebekah, when she "inquires" of God about her pregnancy (Gen. 25:22). God answers her prayer, revealing to her that she is bearing twins who will become two nations (Gen. 25:23). When people inquire of God, this means that they are seeking an answer from God (often through a prophet) about a particular situation (1 Chr. 21:30; 2 Chr. 18:4, 6, 7; 26:5; 34:21, 26). God wants us to seek him for insight and understanding amid all of life's circumstances. People also seek God through his word (1 Chr. 28:8; 2 Chr. 14:4; 17:4), which is not surprising since God's word helps us to understand his will and how we should act. Sometimes people seek answers in things *other* than God, but this does not lead to a positive outcome (1 Chr. 10:13-14; 2 Chr. 16:12). When the verb "to seek, inquire" (*dāraš*) is used with God as its object, people are not simply inquiring about something, but they are seeking God *himself*—he is the object of their pursuit. God had told Moses many years earlier that he would be found by those who seek him (Deut. 4:29), and this verse is recalled in Chronicles. David thus exhorts his son Solomon to seek the LORD, reminding him of this ancient promise (1 Chr. 28:9). Similarly, the prophet Azariah exhorts King Asa and the people to seek the LORD (2 Chr. 14:2, 4). God's people are to search for him with all their heart and with all their soul (Deut. 4:29). This theme of seeking the LORD is seen throughout Chronicles, with echoes of this ancient promise from Deuteronomy reverberating throughout the stories (1 Chr. 28:9; 2 Chr. 14:4; 15:2, 13; 20:3; 26:5, etc.).

The second verb "to seek, search" (*bāqaš*) describes the act of looking for something or someone, such as seeking pasture for flocks (1 Chr. 4:39) or searching for David (1 Chr. 14:8). When dignitaries travel to Jerusalem, they seek "the presence of Solomon" (lit. "the face of Solomon," 2 Chr. 9:23). This same verb "to seek" is used to describe those who seek the LORD (1 Chr. 16:10), or more specifically, those who seek *God's face* (1 Chr. 16:11). Seeking the face of God has the sense of seeking to be in God's presence. When God's *face* shines on his people, it is a sign of his favor and blessing (Num. 6:25). This week we can be encouraged in our pursuit of God because he promises to be found by those who seek him.

Bible Readings
1 Chronicles 16:10-11; 2 Chronicles 14:1-15; 15:1-19; 16:1-14; 17:1-9; 20:1-25

Questions for Reflection
1. Read 1 Chronicles 16:10-11. We begin our study on seeking God by reflecting on two verses that belong to a psalm sung by the Levites after David brings the ark of the covenant into Jerusalem. God's people are exhorted with these words:

Glory in His holy name;
Let the heart of those who seek (*bāqaš*) the LORD be glad.
Seek (*dāraš*) the LORD and His strength;
Seek (*bāqaš*) His face continually. (1 Chr. 16:10-11)

While not evident in our English Bible, the verbs *bāqaš* and *dāraš* in these two verses are plural. This means the psalmist is speaking to a

35

plural audience. Furthermore, the two verbs in verse 11 are imperatives ("commands"). Who is the psalmist addressing (you will need to read 1 Chr. 16:1-9 for the context)? What do these verses teach us about the corporate dimension of seeking God? How might the psalmist's exhortation to seek the LORD *continually* be reflected in our lives and in our corporate worship each Sunday?

2. Read 2 Chronicles 14. How would you characterize Asa's reign in this chapter? What does it mean to "seek the LORD" in this story (*dāraš*, vv. 4, 7)?

3. Asa is described as a king who did what was "good and right" in the sight of God. What does his prayer tell you about his relationship with God (v. 11)? How might you cultivate this kind of dependance upon God in your own life?

4. Read 2 Chronicles 15. The two verbs that we are looking at this week are both used in this chapter (*dāraš*, vv. 2, 12, 13; *bāqaš*, vv. 4, 15). Do the verbs have different meanings or are they essentially the same? How would you characterize seeking God in this chapter?

5. When Asa receives the word of exhortation from the prophet, which includes a warning about the chaos that comes when God's people are without a teaching priest and God's law (vv. 1-7), what action does he take? How might these actions help us understand what it means to seek God both individually and corporately?

6. God's people seek the LORD as they gather for corporate worship (vv. 8-15). How might weekly worship of God at church be a "modern-day equivalent" of what it means to seek God? In our context today, sometimes Christians give priority to events held on Sunday (such as sports, birthday parties, shopping, or even weekends away at a vacation home), resulting in their being absent from church. Would it be fair to describe these as "modern-day equivalents" of failing to seek God wholeheartedly? How does this question challenge you personally?

7. Read 2 Chronicles 16. Asa sought the LORD early in his reign, but what happened to him later in his life? Who did Asa rely on and what message of rebuke did the prophet give him? Identify one or two areas in your own life where you may be tempted to rely on yourself instead of God.

8. A wonderful description of God's providential care for his people is given in the first sentence in verse 9 (another favorite verse of mine in Chronicles!). How might this verse encourage you when you are struggling or feeling weak? Where is strength to be found (see also the first sentence in 1 Chr. 16:11)?

9. The verb "to seek" (*dāraš*) is again used in verse 12. How does this verse serve as a warning to you about becoming complacent in your walk with the Lord? Share one thing you have done in the past few weeks to strengthen your relationship with God or one thing you will do this week.

10. Read 2 Chronicles 17. How would you describe "seeking God" (*dāraš*, vv. 3, 4) in this story? Three actions are noted in verse 4. What are they and how do they contribute to our understanding of what it means to seek God?

11. How does Jehoshaphat's eradication of idolatry (v. 6) and his emphasis on the word of God (vv. 7-9) relate to "seeking God" described earlier? What principles can we learn from the king's actions? How might daily reading of God's word be identified as seeking God?

12. Read 2 Chronicles 20:1-25. Instead of summoning his military when facing an enemy attack, Jehoshaphat seeks the LORD (lit. "he set his face to seek the LORD," *dāraš*, v. 3). What inspires you in this story and what do you find personally challenging?

13. Describe a time in your life when you relied on God amid difficult or overwhelming circumstances. What did you learn from this experience and how might this be an encouragement to others in your group?

14. Are you currently facing a challenging situation? How might this story encourage you to keep trusting in God? Is there a particular verse that is especially meaningful to you?

15. What role does fasting play in this story? Any thoughts on why God's people seek him *and* fast? How might you cultivate this kind of earnest prayer in your own life and in your church community?

16. Notice how the king's actions influenced the people (vv. 3-4, 18). Can you recall a time when someone's godly actions encouraged you to act in a similar manner?

17. In this story, the entire community gathers to seek the LORD (v. 4). What do you think the verb "to seek" (*bāqaš*) means in this situation and how does God answer his people? Can you recall a time when you joined in prayer with other believers in your local church about a challenging situation? What happened?

18. Summarize what you have learned about seeking the LORD from the passages we have studied this week. How is God stirring your heart to draw near to him?

19. What practical steps can you take to deepen your walk with the Lord? Are there any priorities that need to change in your life? Perhaps there's a new habit you might be able to start. Be prepared to share your response with others in your group and pray for each other.

Humbling Oneself

This week we are exploring what it means to "humble oneself." You should be familiar with the well-known verse in Chronicles by now, when God tells Solomon that if his people who are called by his name "humble themselves and pray and seek My face and turn from their wicked ways, then I will hear from heaven, will forgive their sin and will heal their land" (2 Chr. 7:14). The first action of *humbling oneself* emphasizes the kind of posture we are to have before God. But what does this mean practically in our lives? We might initially think it means being a humble person, such as not drawing attention to ourselves or being modest or self-effacing. This kind of humility is certainly a godly virtue, but it is not what is meant by "humbling oneself."

The verb "to subdue, be humbled" (*kāna'*) is used to describe a nation or enemy being "subdued," such as when God "subdues" or "humbles" Israel's enemies who wage war against them (Deut. 9:3; Judg. 3:30; 4:23; 8:28; 1 Sam. 7:13, etc.). This meaning is found in Chronicles when God promises to subdue Israel's enemies (1 Chr. 17:10), and it is used to describe David's subjugation of his enemies (1 Chr. 18:1; 20:4).

But the verb is also used to describe people who humble *themselves* (2 Chr. 7:14; 12:6, 7, 12; 30:11; 32:26; 33:12, 19, 23; 34:27; 36:12). In these cases, it is not God or a king who is doing the action to someone else, but people are humbling *themselves* (the Hebrew verbal form is *reflexive*). Humbling oneself can be described as an internal disposition or posture, a "*self*-humbling." Perhaps it is not surprising to learn that God requires this of his people since this posture recognizes that the LORD alone is God and that we can only draw near to him by his grace. It reminds us that we are utterly dependent upon God for everything. We will learn in our Bible readings this week that humbling oneself can include admitting being wrong (2 Chr. 12:6-7), yielding to the LORD and to his invitation to be reconciled (2 Chr. 30:11), praying to God while in distress (2 Chr. 33:12-13), repenting of one's pride (2 Chr. 32:26), and submitting to God's word (2 Chr. 34:27). Even though people humble themselves in a variety of situations, what is common throughout these stories is the kind of posture they have before God.

The action of self-humbling is an internal disposition of the heart, but it is often demonstrated in outward actions. For example, when Rehoboam is rebuked by a prophet for his wrongdoing, he humbles himself and declares that God is in the right (2 Chr. 12:6). When people from the northern kingdom humble themselves, they yield to the LORD, repent, and return to Jerusalem to celebrate the Passover meal (2 Chr. 30:8-11). When King Josiah hears the word of God and learns that judgment is coming, he tears his clothes and weeps before God, actions that demonstrate his tender and humble heart (2 Chr. 34:19, 27). There are other examples of kings who do not humble themselves, which leads to God's judgment (2 Chr. 33:23; 36:12). In the case of King Zedekiah, it is tragic to read that he fails to humble himself before the prophet Jeremiah, who spoke God's word to him. Instead of yielding to God's word, the king stiffens his neck and hardens his heart, refusing to turn to the LORD. The "stiff-necked" posture of Zedekiah is the opposite of what it means to humble oneself. In our study this week we will reflect on examples in Chronicles where kings and people humble themselves, and we'll look for common characteristics that will help us cultivate this posture before God in our own lives. We want to be people whose hearts are tender and responsive to God's word like Josiah, not like the hard-hearted and stiff-necked Zedekiah, whose life came to ruin.

Bible Readings

2 Chronicles 7:14; 12:1-16; 30:1-27; 32:24-26; 33:1-25; 34:1-33; 36:11-13

Questions for Reflection

1. Read 2 Chronicles 12. The verb "to humble oneself" (*kāna'*) occurs four times in this chapter (vv. 6, 7 [2x], 12). How is Rehoboam described at the beginning of his reign (vv. 1-4)? What happens next? How do Rehoboam and the people respond to the prophet's rebuke (vv. 5-6)?

2. Rehoboam and the people recognize that the LORD was in the right (which implies that they were in the wrong). How willing are you to humble yourself and admit that you are wrong? What kind of posture is required and why is this so difficult?

3. How does God respond when Rehoboam and the people humble themselves (vv. 7-8, 12)? How willing are you to forgive your spouse, friend, or family member after they have apologized? How might your response more closely reflect God's gracious response to Rehoboam and the people?

4. Read 2 Chronicles 30. In this chapter, Hezekiah is king ruling in Jerusalem. It is important to bear in mind that fellow Israelites in the northern kingdom have worshiped foreign gods for over two hundred

years. In their recent history, they have even attacked the southern kingdom and have killed thousands during the reign of Ahaz (see 2 Chr. 28). We pick up the story with Hezekiah inviting the apostate northerners to celebrate the Passover meal in Jerusalem. With this history in view, summarize the setting for the story (vv. 1-9).

5. Hezekiah calls the northerners to return to the LORD, which requires them to repent (vv. 6-9). He exhorts them not to "stiffen their neck" like their forefathers. Having a "stiff neck" (an unyielding posture) is the opposite of humbling oneself. Hezekiah exhorts them to yield to the LORD (literally, to "give a hand" to the LORD), which would indicate a posture of submission. How would you characterize the different responses to Hezekiah's invitation (vv. 10-11)?

6. What would it have felt like for the northerners to have been mocked by their fellow Israelites? Sometimes following a godly path is not received well by others, and it can lead to conflict in relationships, even within one's own family (see Matt. 10:35-37). Has this ever happened to you? How might the Christian community be a support to you when dealing with conflict because of your commitment to follow the Lord?

7. Read 2 Chronicles 32:24-26. We learn in these few verses that Hezekiah's heart becomes proud. What are the circumstances that lead to the king's pride (for more details, see 2 Kgs. 20:1-11)? Are there any areas in your own life that could become a source of unhealthy pride? What is the lesson to be learned in this story?

8. Read 2 Chronicles 33. How would you characterize the first part of Manasseh's reign (vv. 1-9)? Sometimes we can (wrongly) assume that kings from the royal tribe of Judah were all godly kings. Does it surprise you to find a king from the promised line of Judah described in this way?

9. How did God get Manasseh's attention and how did the king respond while in Babylon (vv. 10-12)? How might this story encourage you to confess your sins to God when you have messed up or done something wrong that you are embarrassed about? In what way does God's gracious restoration of a sinful king like Manasseh remind you of a father's love and forgiveness of a prodigal son (see Luke 15:11-32)?

10. Identify a time in your life when God used difficult circumstances to get your attention or bring you to your knees? Although we should not assume that challenging times are due to God's discipline (the Bible gives a variety of reasons), God can use trials to produce godly virtues in us (see Jas. 1:2-4). What spiritual lessons did you learn from your difficult experience?

11. How might the story of Manasseh help you to pray for family members or friends who are not following God or who are "prodigals" in distress? How might you see God at work in their lives? Share with your group someone you are praying for who needs the Lord and take a few moments in your small group to pray for this person.

12. What does Manasseh do after he returns to Jerusalem and how might this demonstrate his genuine repentance (vv. 15-16)? How does God's restoration of Manasseh become a blessing to others in the covenant community?

13. Read 2 Chronicles 34. Josiah seeks God early in his life, which leads him to eradicate idolatry from the land. When his officials are in the temple collecting contributions given by the people, they find the book of the law (v. 14). How does Josiah respond when God's word is read to him (vv. 19-21)?

14. Josiah's actions reveal his posture before God (v. 27). What emotions are seen in this story? Can you think of a time in your own life when you wept or were deeply moved after reading God's word? As Christians, how do we account for this emotional response to an ancient book written thousands of years ago? Can you think of a Bible verse that describes the active role of God's word?

15. The word of God read to Josiah directly impacts his actions (vv. 31-33). As Christians, we are not only to be hearers of God's word but *doers* of the word (see Jas. 1:22). What habits are you cultivating to ensure that you are reading God's word daily, and how are your actions ("what you do") becoming more closely aligned with Scripture as a result? Give a few concrete examples.

16. Read 2 Chronicles 36:11-13. We've read about kings who humble themselves, but we now turn to our last king of the southern kingdom, Zedekiah. Tragically, instead of submitting to God's word through the prophet Jeremiah, we encounter a hard-hearted and stiff-necked king. Jeremiah had repeatedly warned Zedekiah of the impending judgment, but he had refused to listen (see Jer. 37:1-10, 21). What leads to this kind of hard-heartedness and what do *we* need to do to ensure our heart remains tender toward the Lord?

17. In our church context today, pastors and elders have authority to preach and teach God's word. How receptive are you to receive a word of correction through the preaching of God's word? Are there certain teachings of Scripture that you find more difficult to follow than others?

18. Read 2 Chronicles 7:14. We now return to our theme verse. What do you think it means to "humble yourself" in this passage. Why do you think it comes *first* in the list of actions God requires of his people? How might you cultivate humility in your own walk with the Lord and in your relationship with others?

WEEK 5

Listening to Wise Counsel

This week we are considering what it means to listen to wise counsel, which requires a posture of humility. Throughout the period of the monarchy, God raises up counselors and prophets to give wise counsel to Israel's kings and his people. We will see shortly that the success or failure of a king is often directly related to his response to wise counsel. Early in Israel's history, a man named Jethro had "counseled" (*yā'aṣ*, sounds like *ya-ats*) his son-in-law Moses, advising him to appoint leaders to assist him in his leadership responsibilities (Exod. 18:17-27). Moses had wisely listened to his father-in-law, and elders were appointed as a result. In Chronicles, several people are identified as wise counselors, such as Zechariah, known for his insight (1 Chr. 26:14), David's uncle, Jonathan, who was a man of understanding (1 Chr. 27:32), and Ahithophel, who was a counselor to King David (1 Chr. 27:33). By way of contrast, Ahaziah's ungodly mother Athaliah was his counselor, and she counseled him to do evil, following the ways of the apostate northern kingdom (2 Chr. 22:3-4). The danger of not listening to wise counsel is especially seen in the reign of Solomon's son Rehoboam, who foolishly rejects the counsel of wise elders, preferring to take advice from his young friends. In this story, the verb "to counsel" (*yā 'aṣ*) occurs six times (2 Chr. 10:6 [2x], 8 [2x], 9), and the noun "counsel" (*'eṣāh*, sounds like *ets-ah*), which is from the same root, occurs three times (2 Chr. 10:8, 13, 14). Rehoboam's failure to listen to wise counsel has disastrous consequences for the king and the kingdom.

Godly counsel is also given by prophets inspired by God's Spirit to speak his word. The Scriptures teach that God uses prophets and other people to instruct his people in how they are to walk, and that his "counsel" stands. The Chronicler records times when prophets give a word of rebuke or encouragement to kings and the people. For example, the prophet Shemaiah rebukes Rehoboam for forsaking the LORD, and the king responds in repentance (2 Chr. 12:5-8); the prophet Azariah warns Asa about not forsaking the LORD, and the king initiates religious reforms (2 Chr. 15:1-19); Hanani the prophet rebukes Asa for relying on a foreign king, but the king responds in rage (2 Chr. 16:7-10); the prophet Jehu rebukes Jehoshaphat for his alliance with Ahab, and the king establishes reforms in the kingdom (2 Chr. 19:1-11); Jahaziel encourages Jehoshaphat and the people to trust in the LORD, and they respond in faith as they go into battle (2 Chr. 20:14-25); the prophet Zechariah rebukes Joash for transgressing God's commands, but the king does not give heed and judgment is forthcoming (2 Chr. 24:20-27); a prophet rebukes Amaziah, but in his pride the king does not listen (2 Chr. 25:14-20); and eighty priests rebuke Uzziah for entering the temple, but the king refuses to listen and leprosy breaks out on him (2 Chr. 26:16-21). Giving heed to a prophet or prophetess requires humility and a willingness to submit to God's word.

When a rebuke is received, it is often accompanied by repentance and a change of behavior. As an example, Huldah the prophetess speaks God's word to Josiah, making known that judgment is coming upon Judah because of their sin. Josiah not only humbles himself and gives heed to God's word, but he eradicates idolatrous worship practices in the land, and the people recommit themselves to follow God's ways (2 Chr. 34). This story underscores that listening to wise counsel does not simply mean *hearing* what is said, but *giving heed*, which results in a change of behavior or a new course of action.

The stories of Israel's kings in Chronicles remind us that the king and the people are prone to rebel against God or act contrary to his will, but God does not leave them to their own devices. He consistently sends his messengers to call his people back to himself and to keep them on a godly path. We, too, can rebel against God or perhaps even find ourselves drifting away him and his word. For some, daily reading of the Scriptures and active involvement in a local church are no longer a priority. But the stories we will encounter this week teach us that godliness is cultivated in the covenant community and that God uses others to keep us on a godly path. We not only need each other for encouragement and prayer, but also for correction and rebuke. This takes place in the church community, and it reminds us that there are no solo Christians. As you do the readings this week, ask the Holy Spirit to give you a tender heart toward God so that you might willingly yield and be open to receive wise counsel from others.

Bible Readings
2 Chronicles 10:1-19; 12:1-16; 16:7-14; 25:14-20; 26:1-23; 34:1-33

Questions for Reflection
1. Read 2 Chronicles 10. We are returning to the story of Solomon's

son, Rehoboam, as we reflect on the counsel he is given. What is the dilemma facing the king early in his reign (vv. 1-4)?

2. See if you can identify the verb "to give counsel, advice" in this story (*yā'aṣ*, vv. 6 [2x], 8 [2x], 9), along with the noun "counsel" (*'eṣāh*, vv. 8, 13, 14). What do you notice about the counsel given by the elders (vv. 6-7) in comparison to the advice given by the young men (vv. 10-11)? How would you characterize the different advice given? How does Rehoboam respond and why?

	Elders	Young Men
Relationship to Rehoboam		
Counsel Given to Rehoboam		
Character/Qualities of the People Giving Advice		
Rehoboam's Response		

3. When facing a difficult situation or dilemma, who do you consult for counsel? Does a person's age or character influence your choice? What other factors might be taken into consideration when seeking wise counsel? Sometimes we can receive different or conflicting advice. How might you discern what *God* wants you to do in a particular situation?

4. Read 2 Chronicles 12. The story of Rehoboam continues in this chapter. Notice that when the king becomes strong, he and the people forsake the LORD (v. 1). We have seen that strength can be dangerous since it allows us to rely on ourselves instead of God, and this is precisely what we see in this story. But God sends an Egyptian king named Shishak against Jerusalem (vv. 2-4). What word of rebuke does the prophet give to Rehoboam and his princes?

5. How do Rehoboam and the princes respond, and what does God do as a result (vv. 5-8)? Can you think of a time in your own life when you received a word of rebuke or correction from someone (it could be from a spouse, friend, family member, or someone in your church) that required you to humble yourself and admit you were wrong?

6. Read 2 Chronicles 16:7-14. We have already studied Asa, but we are now reflecting on what happens when kings do *not* give heed to a word of rebuke. Notice that Hanani the prophet speaks rather forthrightly to Asa. How might a failure to submit to a rebuke impact a person's character and actions? Perhaps you can recall a time when *you* refused to change or admit you were wrong. How can we avoid this kind of unwillingness to receive a word of rebuke or correction in our own lives?

7. Receiving a word of rebuke is not easy. Think for a moment about this example: Imagine that you are a member of a local church, but you've not been attending church regularly. How would you feel if someone from your church (a pastor, elder, or close friend) held you accountable? Would you be willing to accept their word of correction, or would you get angry with them? Would it result in a change of behavior? What if someone in your church confronted you about gossiping, how would you respond?

8. Read 2 Chronicles 25:14-20. Amaziah has just defeated the Edomites (his use of excessive force, which has its own negative consequences, already hints at his ungodly character; vv. 5-13). A prophet rebukes Amaziah for his idolatry, but in pride he questions whether a prophet has the right to give *him* counsel (he's the king, after all!). The verb "to counsel" (*yāʿaṣ*) appears in the story (vv. 16-17), along with the noun "counsel" (*ʿeṣāh*, v. 16). How does the king respond not only to the message but to the messenger? Why is it that correction can quickly invoke anger in us?

9. How is Amaziah's hubris seen in the parable given by the northern king Joash (vv. 18-19)? The book of Proverbs teaches that pride goes before a fall (Prov. 16:18). How does pride give us an inflated view of ourselves and cause us to reject wise counsel?

10. How might God use fellow believers in your church to hold you accountable? Do you have a good friend who would be willing to confront you if you were becoming proud or if they saw an "ungodly" character trait in you?

11. Read 2 Chronicles 26. Uzziah's reign begins positively. How would you describe the early years of his flourishing kingdom (vv. 4-5)?

12. What were Uzziah's accomplishments that led to his pride (vv. 6-15)? Why is pride so dangerous in our relationships, especially in our relationship with God? How might our success lead to an inflated view of ourselves that can be counter-productive to godliness?

13. How does Uzziah's pride prevent him from giving heed to the advice of eighty priests (vv. 16-22)? What stands out to you in this story?

14. Read 2 Chronicles 34. We have already studied Josiah, but this week our focus is on his response to the word of God through Huldah the prophetess. How would you describe the character of Josiah and his actions during the earlier years of his reign (vv. 1-7)? What godly habits did Josiah establish in his youth that nurtured his tender heart toward the LORD?

15. Describe what happens in the eighteenth year of Josiah's reign, which is dated to 622 BC (vv. 8-18).

16. How does Josiah respond to the word of God and what happens next (vv. 19-33)? Repentance involves a change in behavior. What changes are seen in this story?

17. Josiah's actions tell us about his character. Sometimes we might assume that only women cry, but what causes Josiah to weep in this story? What do his outward emotions tell you about his inward disposition of heart toward God and his word?

18. We have seen in our study this week that God uses his servants to give wise counsel to others who need it. How might you be a wise counselor to someone in your church community? Is there someone you could come alongside to encourage?

19. Has the Holy Spirit convicted you of anything this week that requires repentance and a change of behavior? Perhaps it concerns what you've been watching on TV or on the internet, or it may be unresolved anger with your spouse. Whatever it is, take the step this week to share honestly with your group (or with someone in your group if it requires confidentiality) so that they might pray for you. Ask the Holy Spirit to do his sanctifying work in your life and remember that God is gracious and forgiving.

WEEK 6

Seeking God's Help

This week we are reflecting on what it means to seek God's help in all of life's circumstances. This is another important topic in Chronicles taught in short sermonettes and in longer sections when kings desperately cry out to God. You may be familiar with the popular saying, "God helps those who help themselves." According to a 2017 Gallup Poll, more than fifty percent of Christians believe that this saying is in the Bible (it is not!). It was written in the 1600s by an English politician (its roots can be traced back to Greek mythology), but it was popularized by Benjamin Franklin. While this proverbial saying might seem harmless, it gets the heart of the problem—God promises to help those who *cry out to him* for help. He helps us in our *weakness*. God does not want us to trust in ourselves, but we are to rely upon him. This week we are learning about kings and people who call out to God for help.

The first verb used when people turn to God for help is "to call, proclaim" (*qārā'*). It first occurs in the well-known prayer of Jabez, when a man named Jabez calls out to God amid his pain (1 Chr. 4:9-10). Contrary to a popular teaching (known as the "Prayer of Jabez"), this prayer is not intended to be repeated each day to achieve success or to "enlarge your border." In fact, the Chronicler's own circumstances remind us of the difficulties facing God's people (and they had limited geographical borders!). Although the prayer is no guarantee of success, it serves as an encouragement that God's people are to call out to him amid painful circumstances (cf. 1 Chr. 21:26; 2 Chr. 14:11). We learn in these stories that God answers prayer, and he responds in accordance with his good and perfect will.

The second verb used when people turn to God for help is "to cry out, call out" (*zāʿaq*). Embedded in one of the genealogies is the story of men from northern tribes who "cry out" to God amid a fierce battle. God answers their prayer because they trust in him (1 Chr. 5:20). This is precisely what Jehoshaphat does when facing an enemy attack, and God answers his prayer (2 Chr. 18:31). Later, Jehoshaphat will recall God's promise that if his people "cry out" to him in their distress, he will hear and deliver (2 Chr. 20:9). Hezekiah and Isaiah the prophet will similarly "cry out" to God in prayer when facing an Assyrian attack (2 Chr. 32:20; cf. Neh 9:4, 28). This week we will focus on times when people cry out to God for help amid insurmountable circumstances.

The third verb used is "to help, support" (*ʿāzar*), which describes people who ask God for help and people who receive help (1 Chr. 5:20; 12:1, 17-18; 2 Chr. 14:11; 18:31; 25:8; 26:7; 32:8). In Chronicles we learn that God's people call out to him for help, especially when facing an attack from an enemy. Military battles in the Old Testament were part of the curriculum of life for Israel. God's people were often outnumbered and powerless, but God uses their desperate circumstances so that they might learn to call out to him for help. God uses their weakness so that they might rely on his strength. This is what Asa learns when he calls out to God for help: "LORD, there is no one besides You to help in the battle between the powerful and those who have no strength; so help us, O LORD our God, for we trust in You, and in Your name have come against this multitude" (2 Chr. 14:11).

This is what Jehoshaphat learns when he cries out to God amid the battle (2 Chr. 18:31), causing him to acknowledge later that he was powerless before the great multitude coming against him, but his eyes were on God (2 Chr. 20:12). Encouragement comes through the Spirit of the LORD, when he speaks through Jahaziel, reminding the king and the people that the battle was God's. They were to understand that God would fight on their behalf and that *he* was with them (2 Chr. 20:17). Throughout the Old Testament, God's people were not to rely on their military strength, which could include weapons, horses, chariots, or a large army, but on God alone. We, too, are not to rely on anything other than God. Remember that Chronicles was not simply written as a history book, but the stories of Israel's kings are intended to illustrate godly principles that can be applied to our lives today.

Bible Readings
1 Chronicles 4:9-10; 5:18-20; 12:1-22; 2 Chronicles 14:1-15; 16:1-10; 20:1-25; 32:1-23

Questions for Reflection
1. Read 1 Chronicles 4:9-10. The well-known "prayer of Jabez" has led some to (wrongly) assume that God is promising a pain-free life. Some people think that Christians can receive blessings from God simply by reciting this prayer, but this is not what it means. Remember that the returnees were facing many difficulties—they didn't have a pain-free life and they had limited borders. Keeping this in mind, why do you think this prayer was included in Chronicles and what can we learn from it?

2. Read 1 Chronicles 5:18-22. Another "mini sermon" has been embedded in Reuben's genealogy. What do God's people (from the tribes of Reuben, Gad, and Manasseh) do amid the battle and how does God respond (v. 20)? What is the lesson to be learned from this "mini sermon"?

3. The verb "to cry out" (*zāʿaq*) used in this story (v. 20) occurs elsewhere in Chronicles, such as when Jehoshaphat "cries out" to God for help (2 Chr. 18:31; 20:9), and when Hezekiah and Isaiah "cry out" to God in prayer amid an Assyrian attack (2 Chr. 32:20; cf. Neh. 9:4, 28). How would you describe what it means to "cry out" to God in prayer and how is it different from the prayer of dedication offered by Solomon (2 Chr. 6)? Have you ever prayed this kind of prayer? What were the circumstances and what happened?

4. What does it mean to trust in God *while fighting* the battle (1 Chr. 5:20)? Have there been times in your life when you have taken active steps, while at the same time trusting God to help you? Is it possible for action and prayer to work together? How do you discern when to trust in God *and* act, or when to *refrain* from action and simply trust God to work on your behalf (both situations are found in Chronicles)?

5. Read 1 Chronicles 12:1-22. We have already studied King David, but this story recalls an earlier period in his life before he became king. David had faced many difficult years while fleeing from Saul. During this time, he had even fled to the Philistines and had lived at a town called Ziklag (see 1 Sam. 27). The Chronicler recalls that when David was at Ziklag, men from various tribes came to help him. The verb "to help" (*'āzar*) occurs seven times in the chapter (vv. 12:1, 17, 18 [2x], 19, 21, 22). In what tangible way is David being helped?

6. Several of the men's names reinforce the help David receives: Ahi-*ezer* ("my brother is my help," v. 3), *Azar*-el ("God has helped," v. 6), Jo-*ezer* ("Helper," v. 6), and *Ezer* ("Helper," v. 9). You'll notice that the portion of the name that reflects the Hebrew word "help" (*'āzar* or *'ēzer*) has been put in italics and hyphenated. Reflect on what God is doing in David's life at his time of need. How open are you to receiving help from others in your church community?

7. The Spirit of God gives David spiritual insight, enabling him to interpret his circumstances from *God's* perspective. Who is the ultimate source of David's help (v. 18)? Why is spiritual insight needed to discern what God *is* doing and how he *is* present, especially when we might feel abandoned by God? How is this kind of "spiritual insight" given to us today?

8. Can you recall a time in your life when a friend or someone from your church helped you with something or did something kind that was meaningful to you? You may not even have asked for help, but *God knew* you needed it, and he brought someone to help you. How might the story of David encourage you to reflect on God's providential care in your life and in the lives of others, even when it might not be readily apparent?

9. Read 2 Chronicles 14. We have already encountered this story, but we are now looking at Asa's response when he was outnumbered by a large army. How would you describe the early days of Asa's reign (vv. 1-7)?

10. What does the king do when he hears the news that a large army is marching toward Jerusalem (v. 11)? Who is the source of Asa's help? We often think that God helps those who help themselves, but how does Asa describe *his* situation? What does it mean practically for Asa and the people to trust in God?

11. While we do not face military opposition like Asa did, nor does God promise military victory as he did to Israel under the old covenant (since we are under the new covenant), the Scriptures exhort us not to put our trust in things other than God (whether our achievements, abilities, wealth, retirement accounts, or even past successes), but we are to put our trust in God alone. What do you do when you are struggling with an issue or feeling overwhelmed by circumstances? What is one "take away" from this story?

12. Read 2 Chronicles 16:1-10. Asa is attacked by a northern king, but instead of turning to God for help, he foolishly forges a military alliance with a foreign nation and seeks their help. His military strategy was very successful (vv. 4-6), but the prophet Hanani rebukes the king (vv. 7-9). Sometimes we can think that "the end justifies the means," but what does this story teach us about success achieved by ungodly means?

13. Read 2 Chronicles 20:1-25. Earlier in his reign, Jehoshaphat had foolishly forged an alliance with an ungodly northern king named Ahab (see 2 Chr. 18). Even though he had been warned of military defeat by a prophet, Jehoshaphat had foolishly gone to battle. Yet amid the battle, he had "cried out" (*zā'aq*) and the Lord had "helped" (*'āzar*) him (2 Chr. 18:31). Now consider the king's prayer in *this* chapter. How might God's *past* deliverance in his life (18:31) and in Israel's history (20:7, 10) give Jehoshaphat and the people courage to trust God in their *present* circumstances?

14. Jehoshaphat was not afraid to acknowledge his own fears and his utter powerlessness (vv. 3, 12). What role does weakness play in the story and how is God using it in Jehoshaphat's life?

15. Reflect for a few minutes on your strengths and weaknesses. In what way do your strengths adversely impact your relationship with God? How might God use weakness in your life to cause you to rely upon him?

16. Jehoshaphat exhorts the people to put their trust in the Lord their God amid overwhelming circumstances (v. 20). They are required to believe in the Lord, just like Abraham had done many years ago (cf. Gen. 15:6). The Bible teaches that without faith it is impossible to please God (Heb. 11:6). How do Jehoshaphat and the people demonstrate their faith in the Lord? Describe a situation you are currently facing in your life that requires you to have faith in God, despite the circumstances.

17. Read 2 Chronicles 32:1-23. The Assyrians attack Jerusalem in 701 BC during the reign of Hezekiah. A fierce battle is being fought at the nearby city of Lachish where God's people suffer a terrible defeat. In the meantime, Hezekiah secures the water supply and prepares for battle (vv. 1-6), but he then exhorts the people to be strong and courageous (v. 7). What does Hezekiah say about God to encourage the people? List some of God's attributes that Hezekiah mentions to build the people's faith and to alleviate their fear.

18. Can you think of a difficult time in your life when someone encouraged you to rely upon God and reminded you of God's character or his promises? How did you respond?

19. While we do not face military battles like Israel did in the Old Testament, what "spiritual weapons" did God's people use, and what principles can we learn from this story (see also Eph. 6:10-17)?

20. Notice that Hezekiah and Isaiah both pray (v. 20; cf. Isa. 37:14-20). Do you have others in your church who pray *for* you and *with* you? How might you foster spiritual friendships with people in your church or Bible study group? Take time to pray for each other in your small group this week.

WEEK 7

Giving Generously

This week we are studying the topic of generosity. Before looking at passages in Chronicles, it is helpful to consider how God's people in the Old Testament were expected to use their resources. When the tabernacle was built during Israel's early years, God had instructed Moses to raise contributions "from everyone whose heart prompts them to give" (Exod. 25:2, NIV). At that time, God's people gave willingly toward the tabernacle, not out of obligation or compulsion. Similarly, freewill offerings are given during the reign of David when the people "give willingly" toward the construction of the temple (*nādab,* 1 Chr. 29:5, 6, 9, 14, 17). Their generosity recalls the time when the people had freely given gifts toward the tabernacle (*nādab,* Exod. 25:2; 35:21, 29). The voluntary nature of these gifts and the generosity of the people are seen in the story of David, as hearts are moved to give freely to the LORD. David first gives generously from his treasures, and his leaders follow his example, bringing great joy to the entire community (1 Chr. 29:9). This story challenges us to consider how we are using our resources for God's kingdom.

The Israelites were required to set aside the tithe. Ten percent of their agricultural produce was given to the Levites (the Old Testament equivalent of clergy) for their service in the tabernacle and later temple. The Levites served as worship leaders, musicians, teachers of the Scriptures, gate-keepers, and trusted guardians of the temple treasuries. Since the Levites were not assigned an allotment of land like other tribes, they relied upon tithes for their livelihood (Deut. 18:1-8). Accordingly, every Israelite was required to give a tithe to compensate the Levites for their service (Num. 18:21-32). The tithe was also set aside for the poor, widow, and orphan (Deut. 14:27-29). Even the Levites were not exempt from the tithe-law since their tithes provided for Israel's priests (Num. 18:28; Neh. 10:35-39; 12:47). Underlying the tithe-law was God's generous gift of land and its abundance. There was the expectation, therefore, that God's people would reciprocate by giving generously and sacrificially to the LORD through their tithes and freewill offerings. This week we will learn about Hezekiah when he requires the tithe so that the Levites can devote themselves to the law of God (2 Chr. 31:4-6). When their gifts are received, the king is overjoyed to see the generosity of God's people, and there is even a large amount left over.

The Jerusalem Temple also required daily maintenance and upkeep. Supplies were needed so that Israel's priests and Levites could conduct daily worship. During the time of Moses, Israelites twenty years and older were required to give an annual contribution toward the tabernacle (Exod. 30:12-16; 38:25-26). This "temple tax" was required of every Israelite, whether rich or poor, as it was needed for the upkeep and maintenance of the tabernacle (and later temple). Over time, contributions were necessary for repairs, and this was especially urgent during years of neglect when ungodly kings failed to upkeep the temple. Sometimes, they even closed the temple doors. We will learn that Joash issues a command that every Israelite contribute to the temple so that it might be repaired (2 Chr. 24:4-5), and contributions for repairs are also needed during the reign of Josiah (2 Chr. 34:8-10).

Like ancient Israel, our tithes and offerings given to the Lord are used to support those in full-time ministry, whether preachers, teachers, worship leaders, or other church leaders and staff. Just as Moses warned the Israelites not to neglect the Levite in their midst (Deut. 14:27), we, too, are not to neglect those serving the Lord, ensuring that pastors and ministry leaders receive adequate compensation for their service. Like ancient Israel, our gifts are needed for the maintenance of church buildings, parsonages, and church grounds. Freewill contributions are required for specific building projects or deferred maintenance. The principle of giving to the Lord is rooted in the Old Testament concept that everything belongs to God and that he has provided abundantly for his people. As you read the stories in Chronicles this week about giving and generosity, keep in mind the various requirements and expectations of giving in the Old Testament. May God stir your heart to be generous, not out of obligation or compulsion but out of gratitude for all that God has done for you.

Bible Readings

1 Chronicles 21:18-25; 22:11-19; 29:1-30; 2 Chronicles 9:1-31; 24:1-14; 31:1-21

Questions for Reflection

1. Read 1 Chronicles 21:18-25. David had sinned against God when he had conducted a military census (he had counted his army instead of trusting in God). This invokes God's wrath, but David is instructed to build an altar to the Lord on the threshing floor of Ornan (also known as Araunah). Ornan graciously offers to give David the threshing floor, along with the animals for the burnt offerings, but David refuses. He

states emphatically that he will not give to the Lord that which costs him nothing (v. 24). What does David do instead?

2. Sometimes people "repackage" a gift that someone has given them. Does this make you feel uneasy? What is wrong with it and how might "regifting" help us to understand David's insistence that *he* had to pay for the threshing floor, along with the sacrifice he was offering to God?

3. You might have heard the popular saying, "Show me your checkbook and I'll tell you your values." What does your checkbook, bank account, or the budgeting app on your phone say about you? Can you think of any New Testament passage where Jesus underscores the importance of sacrificial giving?

4. Read 1 Chronicles 22:11-19. David generously gives his gold, silver, bronze, and iron toward the temple that his son Solomon will build (David will not even get the credit for the building!). With "great pains" David makes preparations for the temple to ensure that it is well-supplied and beautifully adorned with precious materials. David's generosity is an outward demonstration of his priorities and what is important to him. As you reflect on your own life, prayerfully consider how God might want you to use your time, talents, and financial resources for his kingdom-work. Be specific. What steps could you take so that your life is characterized by service and giving to God?

5. Read 1 Chronicles 29. David has devoted his time, talents, and resources for the establishment of the kingdom in anticipation of Solomon's reign. When he invites his leaders to give, he summons those who have willingly consecrated themselves to the Lord (v. 5). Consecration in this story means being set apart for God. How is giving financial resources connected to our devotion to the Lord, and why does David ask his leaders to dedicate themselves *first* to the Lord before they give their resources (see also 2 Cor. 8:3-5)?

6. As noted earlier, the verb "to be willing, to willingly offer" (*nāḏaḇ*) occurs seven times in this chapter (vv. 5, 6, 9 [2x], 14, 17 [2x]). See if you can identify the verbs in your English Bible (translations may vary, but the same Hebrew verb is used). Who is the subject of each verb? What else do you notice about this story that demonstrates the people's devotion to the Lord?

   v. 5

   v. 6

v. 9

v. 14

v. 17

7. How does David's theology (reflected in his prayer) impact how he uses his resources (vv. 11-17)? List some of his theological convictions that lead him to give generously.

8. What is your "theology of giving" and how does it impact how you use your financial resources? Where does your theology come from and how is it displayed in your life?

9. In this story, people rejoice over the generosity of others. Have you ever been part of a ministry project or fund-raising effort that involved the wider Christian community? How has the generosity of others encouraged you to be generous? Give an example of someone else's generosity that has impacted you.

10. Read 2 Chronicles 9. How does this chapter describing Solomon's final years compare with the chapter describing David's final years (1 Chr. 29)? Compare and contrast these two kings. What do you notice about them that might give insight into their relationship with God and their values (more information about Solomon is given in 1 Kgs. 11:1-13; his idolatry is not mentioned in Chronicles)? How do their lives compare to your own walk with the Lord and your values? Which king are you more like? Why?

	David	Solomon	My life
How are gold, silver, and precious goods being used?			
Who is being honored?			
Evidence of a "God-focused" life or "self-focused" life?			

11. What kind of spiritual qualities do you need to cultivate *now* so that you might leave a godly legacy at the end of your life? If you were writing your own epitaph, what would you want people to say about you?

12. Reflecting further on the topic of a leaving a legacy, have you ever considered "legacy giving," which entails leaving a financial gift, stocks, or property to a church or Christian organization in your will? How might David's use of his resources at the end of his life be comparable to "legacy giving"?

13. Read 2 Chronicles 24:1-14. During the reign of Joash, the temple needed to be repaired since it had been neglected and misused under the ungodly rule of Athaliah (v. 7). The Levites collect a mandatory temple tax to be used for the upkeep and maintenance of the temple (cf. Exod. 30:12-16). Who is responsible for the repairs to the temple and how are the contributions collected?

14. What is the difference between "freewill offerings" (as in 1 Chr. 29) and the "temple tax" required of every Israelite (as in 2 Chr. 24)? How might these two types of gifts be reflected in your church?

15. If your church building needs to be repaired or restored (perhaps due to deferred maintenance or an aging property), how might this story challenge you and how might you respond? What does this chapter teach us about the responsibility of the whole church to ensure that church buildings and property are well-maintained?

16. Read 2 Chronicles 31. Hezekiah requires that the tithe be given so that the Levites might devote themselves to the study of the Scriptures. The Levites had been set aside as teachers of God's word (see 2 Chr. 17:7-9), and the covenant community was responsible for their livelihood so that they could study God's word and teach it to others (see Ezra 7:10). How is generosity reflected in this story and what happens as a result?

17. Moses had warned the Israelites not to neglect the Levites in their town (see Deut. 14:27). How might the principle of the tithe given to the Levites be applicable for church leaders today? Is your pastor neglected or well-cared for? How might your church (and you personally) better care for your pastor and ministry leaders?

18. Spend time mediating on 1 Chronicles 29:11-17. What might the Holy Spirit be saying to you through your Bible readings this week? What has been most challenging for you? Are there any priorities that need to change so that you can be better aligned with God's kingdom?

WEEK 8

Singing Joyfully to God

The final topic in our Bible study on *Cultivating Godliness* is singing joyfully to God. This week we are reflecting on the worship practices of ancient Israel so that our lives might be filled with joyful worship as part of our daily rhythm. The Israelites had sung a song of praise to the LORD when he had delivered them out of bondage in Egypt (Exod. 15:1-21). Aaron's sister Miriam, along with other women, had worshiped the LORD with timbrels and with dancing—it was a joyous occasion as they sang to the LORD! From Israel's earliest days there was the expectation that God's people would praise him and sing joyfully at the place where his name would dwell (Deut. 12:7, 12, 18). This chapter in Deuteronomy anticipates that praises will be sung in the temple, the place where God has chosen for his name to dwell. A variety of musical instruments were known in the ancient world, and artifacts depicting musical ensembles show musicians playing the flute, cymbals, lyre, and tambourine. An example of the types of musical instruments played in Israel is seen in the final and climactic psalm which begins with a call to praise God: "Praise the LORD! Praise God in his sanctuary; Praise Him in His mighty expanses. Praise Him for His mighty deeds; Praise Him according to His excellent greatness (Ps. 150:1-2). The psalmist emphasizes that God is to be praised with the trumpet sound, the harp and lyre, with timbrel and dancing, with stringed instruments and pipe, and with loud cymbals (Ps. 150:3-5)! The psalmist concludes: "Let everything that has breath praise the LORD. Praise the LORD!" (Ps. 150:6).

Since the tribe of Levi is set apart to serve in the tabernacle and temple, it is not surprising to find that three musical families, who trace their ancestry back to Aaron, form the basis of Israel's worship leaders: Heman, the singer from the line of Kohath (1 Chr. 6:33-38), Asaph, from the line of Gershon (1 Chr. 6:39-43), and Ethan, from the line of Merari (1 Chr. 6:44-47). Singing praises to God is not only mentioned throughout the psalms, but we find Levites leading God's people in praise and worship throughout Chronicles, and there are even Levitical choirs! In fact, the verb "to sing" (*šiyr*, sounds like *shir*) occurs with high frequency in Chronicles. Levitical singers delight in praising the LORD (2 Chr. 5:12-13; 20:21; 23:13; 29:28). When the ark of the covenant is brought into Jerusalem, David (who is himself a musician) sets apart the Levites to give thanks to God and to sing praises to him (1 Chr. 15:16-26; 16:4-7). The procession of the ark is a joyous occasion as Levitical choirs sing and play their musical instruments in celebration of the LORD (1 Chr. 15:28). Three psalms sung by the Levites are collected into one song of praise (1 Chr. 16). Their joyful singing is accompanied by an array of musical instruments, including harps, lyres, and loud sounding cymbals! When the ark is brought into the newly constructed temple, the Levites again lead Israel in worship, with 120 priests blowing trumpets (2 Chr. 5:11-14)!

In Chronicles, we will find that worship is an occasion of great joy. The noun "joy" (*simḥāh*) occurs three times in the first five books of the Old Testament, known as the Pentateuch (Gen. 31:27; Num. 10:10; Deut. 28:47), two times in 1-2 Samuel (1 Sam. 18:6; 2 Sam. 6:12), once in 1-2 Kings (1 Kgs. 1:40), but twelve times in Chronicles. Just to mention a few examples, there is joy when the ark of the covenant is brought into Jerusalem (1 Chr. 15:16, 25), when people give willingly to the LORD (1 Chr. 29:9, 17, 22), when God defeats Israel's enemies (2 Chr. 20:27), when burnt offerings are offered to God (2 Chr. 23:18), and when God's people celebrate the Passover (2 Chr. 30:21).

As we reflect on this important topic of joyful praise, it is important to remember that during the Chronicler's own time, God's people were living in Israel as a small province amid a vast Persian Empire. They were required to pay heavy taxes to Persia, and some had struggled financially, requiring them to mortgage their property. The returnees occupied a small area of land (the province of Yehud) in comparison to the flourishing kingdom under David and Solomon. Yet, despite their difficult circumstances, the Chronicler is recalling times in their history that had been characterized by joyful praise. God is exhorting us through these stories that we are to praise him and to sing joyfully to him regardless of our circumstances. God is *always* worthy of praise, and worship is filled with joy because of God's presence in our lives.

The theme of joy has been included under the topic of godliness because praising God is not limited to worshiping God in church, but we are to praise God daily. The Levites praised God in the temple morning and evening, and this provides a helpful rhythm for our lives. In the psalm sung when the ark is brought into Jerusalem, the Levites exhort God's people with these words: "Sing to him, sing praise to him; tell of all his wonderful acts" (1 Chr. 16:9), and again in verse 23: "Sing to the LORD, all the earth; proclaim his salvation day after day" (1 Chr. 16:23). We have been set apart as a worshiping and witnessing people of God, and our praises are a testimony to the reality that God is King and Lord of all. He is worthy of praise—*every day*!

Bible Readings
1 Chronicles 15:1-29; 16:1-43; 2 Chronicles 5:11-14; 7:1-10; 20:14-22; 29:20-30; 30:21-27

Questions for Reflection

1. Read 1 Chronicles 15. David had previously attempted to bring the ark of the covenant into Jerusalem (1 Chr. 13), but Uzzah had been killed because God had not been treated as holy (the correct procedures for moving a holy object had not been followed; see Deut. 10:8). In this story, David not only appoints Levites to transport the ark, but they are to give thanks to God and to raise sounds of joy. As you read this chapter, what stands out to you?

2. Notice that David is "leaping and celebrating" on this joyous occasion, but how does Michal respond (vv. 27-29; cf. 2 Sam 6:16, 20-21)? Have you ever felt uncomfortable (or perhaps even had judgmental thoughts) about someone in your church whose posture in worship (such as raising hands, clapping, or dancing) seemed ostentatious to you? What might this story teach you about worship?

3. Read 1 Chronicles 16. The psalm sung by the Levites is a collection of three psalms (Pss. 96:1-13; 105:1-15; 106:1, 47-48), with each literary unit beginning with a word of exhortation: "Give thanks to the Lord" (1 Chr. 16:8), "Sing to the Lord, all the earth" (v. 23), and "Give thanks to the Lord" (v. 34). Read the chapter in one sitting. What emotions are stirred in you as you read the psalm? In what way does the psalm focus your attention on God and draw you into worship?

4. Make a list of the things God's people are exhorted *to do* in the first literary unit (vv. 8-22), which begins with exhortation, "Oh give thanks to the Lord" (v. 8).

5. What does it mean to "sing praises *to him*" (v. 9; see also v. 23, "to the Lord")? How is this different from simply singing to ourselves or singing along with the radio? We can sing praises to God at church, at home, in the car, or at any place. How much is singing hymns or songs of praise to the Lord part of your life?

6. The second literary unit begins with the exhortation: "Sing to the Lord all the earth" (v. 23). How is God described in this section and what are God's people to proclaim in their worship (vv. 23-33)? How does this psalm compare with contemporary songs of praise?

7. Why is it important to know who God is when we worship him? How might remembering what God has done stir your heart to worship God? Is there something in this psalm that is especially meaningful to you?

8. The third literary unit begins with the exhortation: "O give thanks to the Lord, for He is good" (v. 34). The psalm then concludes with thanksgiving, and all the people say "Amen" and praise the Lord (v. 36). What happens next? What can you learn from these final verses about worship in ancient Israel (vv. 37-43)? How might the "morning and evening" rhythm of offerings and thanksgiving be reflected in your relationship with the Lord?

9. Read 2 Chronicles 5:11-14 and 7:1-10. Israel's priests bring the ark of the covenant into the newly constructed temple (5:7-10). When the priests come out of the temple, what happens next? Describe the scene in this story (5:11-14) and later after the temple has been dedicated (7:1-10). What emotions would these scenes have stirred in God's people? What is the source of the people's joy?

10. How would you describe your relationship with God? Is joyful praise part of your relationship with God, or would you say that it lacks joy?

11. We have been focusing on worship in the Old Testament, but it continues in the early church as believers praise God and worship Jesus as Lord (see Eph. 5:19-20; Col. 3:16). How would you compare worship at your church on Sunday to what took place in in ancient Israel and in the early church when they gathered for worship?

Worship in Ancient Israel	Worship in the Early Church	Worship at My Church

12. Read 2 Chronicles 20:14-22. You should be familiar with this story of Jehoshaphat by now (a king beloved by the Chronicler and by this author!). What is the context for praise in this chapter? How does singing praises to God demonstrate faith and trust in him?

13. You may be familiar with the old song that includes the words, "Put on the garment of praise for the spirit of heaviness, lift up your voice to God" (cf. Isa. 61:3). Have you experienced times in your relationship with God when you praised him, even when you were heavy burdened or felt discouraged? Why is it important to praise God during *all* of life's circumstances?

14. What praise song or hymn do you sing when you feel discouraged or defeated? How does it encourage you to focus on God? Share with your group one of your favorite hymns.

15. Read 2 Chronicles 29:20-30. When Hezekiah becomes king, he restores temple worship after the reign of his idolatrous father Ahaz. The king cleanses the temple (vv. 1-19) and priests offer sacrifices to make atonement for Israel (vv. 20-24), but then Hezekiah stations the Levites to lead worship. How would you describe the scene (vv. 25-30)? What stands out to you?

16. Read 2 Chronicles 30:21-27. What does this chapter teach you about the joy experienced when God's people gather together for worship? While not apparent in our English Bible, the Greek translation of the word "assembly" (*qāhāl,* vv. 2, 4, 13, 17, 23-25) is *ekklēsia,* the same word translated as "church" in the New Testament (Matt. 16:18; 18:17; Acts 5:11). The word "church" refers to the *gathering* of believers, not the building. How might this Old Testament background help us to assess "online church," where Christians no longer gather together (physically) with other believers? What are your thoughts on these "virtual" gatherings?

17. How important is gathering for weekly worship to you personally? Are there any priorities that need to change in order to ensure that you gather regularly for worship with other believers?

18. In the Old Testament, worship took place in the temple—the place of God's presence among his people. The atoning work of Jesus has enabled us to draw near to God (see Heb. 10:19-25). This means that we can praise God in our homes, while on a walk, or wherever we are (even in prison, see Acts 16:25), but we are the "church" when we *gather* for worship as one body. Is there any step you might take to ensure that worship is part of your daily and weekly (Sunday) relationship with God?

19. As we conclude our study of 1-2 Chronicles, share with your group what you have learned in this study. How have you been encouraged to cultivate godliness in your own life? How has the Holy Spirit been stirring you to draw closer to God?

Resources for Further Bible Study

I hope that you have grown in your relationship with the Lord through this Bible study. As followers of Jesus, we want to cultivate life-long habits of reading God's word, prayer, worship, fellowship with other believers, and service to the Lord. Studying God's word in small groups is one of the ways we can grow in our faith and deepen our relationship with believers in the local church. If you would like to begin another Bible study, you'll find other Bible studies and resources at the Casket Empty website (www.casketempty.com) and at my own website (www.carolmkaminski.com). My goal is to provide resources for the local church that foster spiritual growth and knowledge of the Scriptures in the lives of believers. I hope this Bible study has been a blessing to you and to your local church.

Guidelines for Leaders

I am delighted that you have decided to study Chronicles. It is a privilege and great blessing to lead a Bible study group. The weekly topics in this Bible study will draw your group deeper into the Scriptures and closer to the Lord. Since this study is in Chronicles, you may feel intimidated by the prospect of leading this study. It can take years of study to feel confident teaching the Old Testament but remember that you do not need to be an expert. Others do not expect you to have all the answers. You are embarking on a journey with fellow believers, as you study God's word *together*. But there are some practical steps you can take ahead of time to prepare for the weekly studies so that you are an effective small group leader.

Getting Started

This Bible study has been designed as a weekly small group study or Bible class. It is important to give a few weeks lead time so that people in your group can order a copy of the Bible study. Having the Bible study ahead of time gives people time to read ahead and familiarize themselves with Chronicles. This also enables you to extend an invitation to others who may not already be part of a small group. Bible study invitation cards that match the cover artwork are available through the website www. casketempty.com, along with other promotional products. You simply need to add your church information and dates for your study, and then have the cards printed at your church or through a local printer.

Weekly Preparation

Each week participants will be reading several chapters from Chronicles and answering questions related to content and application. Spend time prayerfully reading the Bible passages, and if you need to read additional chapters so that you are familiar with the context, it is well worth the effort. Ask God to give insight into his word, and prayerfully consider how the passages apply to your life, using the application questions as a guide. In addition to the Bible readings and questions, one of the best ways you can prepare to lead your Bible study is to read through sections of my commentary on Chronicles: *1-2 Chronicles. The Story of God Bible Commentary* (eds. Tremper Longman III and Scot McKnight; Grand Rapids: Zondervan, 2023). You should begin by reading the commentary sections relevant to the weekly Bible readings. Be sure to read the "Live the Story" section where I discuss areas of application that will be helpful for your Bible study. You will not only gain an in-depth understanding of the weekly lessons by reading the relevant sections of the commentary ahead of time, but this will build confidence in you as a leader. The commentary should be your first "go to" resource, as it functions as a leader's guide for this study. You will benefit by reading additional sections in the commentary to gain a deeper understanding of 1-2 Chronicles.

As noted in the Introduction, the *CASKET EMPTY Old Testament Timeline* is an invaluable resource since it provides a visual overview of Israel's kings. Another resource you will find helpful is my companion volume, *CASKET EMPTY Old Testament Study Guide*, which is available through the Casket

Empty website (www.casketempty.com). You will find the four chapters on the period of Kings (chs. 4-7) especially helpful, along with the period of Temple (ch. 9), which covers the final period of the Old Testament (when Chronicles was written). Lastly, a Study Bible is always a helpful reference tool (such as the ESV or NIV Study Bible). It will give you further insight into specific verses so that you can be prepared for questions that may arise in your small group.

Format for the Study

There are several ways to lead this eight-week Bible study, but it will depend on what format is most suitable for your church context. If you are doing the study in a small group, eight to ten people are ideal, meeting at church or in someone's home. Once the group has gathered and you have welcomed everyone, there are a few options for the first ten to fifteen minutes. One option is to begin each week by inviting feedback from the group about what they have learned during the week, or you could ask people to highlight one thing that has been meaningful to them. The goal is group participation before you dive into the study questions. The advantage of this approach is that you will learn about the felt needs of people in your group, and you may want to shape the discussion as a result. Another approach requires you to take a more active teaching role by providing some introductory comments, perhaps 10-15 minutes. The advantage of this approach is that it gives you an opportunity to review the lesson and give additional content. This is especially helpful for larger groups, as it enables the main leader or pastor to introduce key teaching points before people break into smaller discussion groups.

Depending on the time allocated for your weekly study, you may need to decide ahead of time which questions you will discuss as a group since you may not have time to discuss all of them. Make sure you leave time for people to share about how God's word applies to their lives personally.

Lastly, it is important to conclude your weekly study with a time of prayer. Since this study is about cultivating godliness, it is important that you pray together and for one another. Try to apply what you have learned for the week during the time of prayer, asking God to help with specific areas of application. Praying for one another forms a bond with your group and it fosters community. You may also want to set up prayer partners so that each person is praying for someone else during the week.

As you embark on this study, may the Lord equip you to teach his word, and may you do so in confidence, knowing that God's word is living and active; it will not return empty without accomplishing what he desires. My prayer is that you might grow closer to the Lord through this study and that it will be a blessing to others in your church community.

Carol M. Kaminski

Made in the USA
Las Vegas, NV
11 February 2025

17884603R00069